Athlete of life

Act or be acted upon?

Catalogage avant publication de Bibliothèque et Archives Canada

Schneider, Thierry

Athlete of life: act or be acted upon?

Revised and expanded edition. (Personal development collection)

ISBN-13: 978-2-89225-627-7 ISBN-10: 2-89225-627-5

1. Control (Psychology). 2. Self-development. 3. Self-mastery. 4. Self-confidence. 5. Influence (Psychology). I. Title. II. Collection.

    BF632.S455 2006   153.8   C2006-941292-8

Civic address:
Éditions Un monde différent
3905, rue Isabelle, bureau 101
(Québec) Canada J4Y 2R2
Tél.: 450 656-2660
Website: www.unmondedifferent.com
Email: info@umd.ca

Postal address:
Éditions Un monde différent
C. P. 51546, Succ. Galeries Taschereau
Greenfield Park (Quebec)
J4V 3N8
Fax: 450 659-9328

Legal deposits: 2nd quarter 2007
National Library of Quebec
National Library of Canada
National Library of France

Cover graphic design and page layout:
OLIVIER LASSER

Inside drawings:
LUC NORMANDIN

Typography: Garamond 12 in 15 pts

New revised and expanded edition
Edition revised and optimized with the cooperation of Marc Maillard
ISBN-13 978-2-89225-627-7 (2nd edition, 2006)
EAN 9782892256277
ISBN-10 2-89225-491-4 (1st edition, 2002)

Printed in Canada

DEAR COLLEAGUES

With GF AgieCharmilles a new chapter is beginning in the world of EDM and milling after more than a century of being in existence, a global success on an almost unprecedented scale in the world of machine tools. With over 50,000 machines in service in all industrialized countries the Agie, Charmilles and Mikron makes have a very considerable market value.

We can now see the exchange value of this great endeavor. A value that has supported and still supports tens of thousands of people directly and indirectly across the world. We have a moral and professional obligation to consolidate and develop this industrial heritage without destroying what others have built up over a lifetime of effort in the hope of passing it on to other "entrepreneurs". Nor do we have the right to profit from this industrial heritage without also devoting our own unyielding efforts to it.

The qualities of the men and women who make up GF Agie Charmilles are its greatest asset, the main foundation on which GF AgieCharmilles must build to continue its story.

The extent of future successes will be dependent on the passion and the desire to innovate, to transform all creative initiatives into reality and a success that will mark out the next important stages for the company and the group's technologies on a global level. This passion and this desire must be the common denominator for every person who is a part of the company. They must be active and dynamic in their everyday work like a shockwave energizing the organization, reaching the far corners of the Americas, Europe, Asia, Africa and Oceania.

It is this state of mind that we, as new entrepreneurs, must cultivate so that it becomes clearly perceptible by all the companies, customers, our partners, our suppliers and opinion leaders. The power of this state of mind alone will make the competition crumble and retreat and will forge a new identity for +GF+ AgieCharmilles in a sustainable way.

The 15 May 2007 must mark an epoch in our way of thinking, acting and communicating. It is by using our minds that we can build our future by thinking of solutions. Only in this way will our actions become creative actions with sustainable effects.

We must do today what others will be doing tomorrow. We must do it with a relentless desire to act with the power of an organization that recognizes that only the value of its men and women will allow it to attain and realize its visions.

So let's follow the example of world athletes, sports champions whose ambitions, motivation and vision we can discover through their sporting career at the Olympic Museum of the International Olympic Committee (IOC) and let's all prepare for these big events and challenges that await us in the months and years to come.

In the words of two famous athletes, who have overcome obstacles and great adversity to achieve success:

"One important key to success is self-confidence. An important key to self-confidence is preparation." – Arthur Ashe (Tennis)

"Champions aren't made in gyms, champions are made from something they have deep inside them – a desire, a dream, a vision." – Mohammed Ali

This dream, this vision, lives in all of us insomuch as we are here. From now on let's make this desire become reality and propagate this flame around us, to all come together on 15/05/07 at the IOC and then in September 2007 at EMO (World Exhibition of Machine Tools).

In conclusion, I would like to thank Thierry Schneider and all my team, who, thanks to their creative and positive energy have managed to transform thoughts, desires and emotions into actions that are vital for our success today and in the future.

International Olympic Committee, May 2007
ARMANDO PEREIRA
Marketing & Communications Manager
+GF+ AgieCharmilles

I dedicate this book to two very dear friends, true "Athletes of Life".
To you, dear Irina Arm, who helped me discover the twilight.
My words will always be empowered
by our rich Californian exchanges.

To you, my dear Martin Helbach, with whom I have shared
the depth and richness of simple moments of happiness.
You resonate with authenticity
through my expression.

As well as to Jean-Jacques Lanoy, a touching and engaging
individual, who has always dedicated himself to Humanity,
with a capital H, and of which he has so often
enthusiastically reminded us all.

You will always be true "Athletes of Life" and your presence lights
my way despite your absence...

Thank you!

According to Peter Drucker,
a manager has only one person
to manage: himself.

Thierry Schneider

Athlete of Life

Act or be acted upon?

PREFACE OF MIKE HORN

UN MONDE 👫 DIFFÉRENT

TABLE OF CONTENTS

FOREWORD

A few years ago, a friend suggested that I take part in a joint book project on goalkeeper instructors. He asked me to describe the "key ideas" I had developed during my days as a soccer goalie and as a coach.

Enriched by this endeavor and encouraged by a growing demand from my readers for a book about my approach to coaching, I finally made up my mind when I confirmed my participation in "Success 2002"[1], which brought together a wide range of speakers. I decided to adapt these universal principles so people could use them in any professional activity. Thus, the *Athlete of Life* project was born and now this second updated, expanded and enhanced edition has been released.

Life has been extremely generous to me, offering many opportunities for discovery and personal growth in soccer, physical fitness, prevention and coaching. I am also grateful for the inspiring experiences I have had through sharing, teaching, and research, as well as the highs and lows that made it possible to write this guide, which is for you who have the courage, here and now...

- to take responsibility for your life, your path;
- to escape from the conventional in order to invent tomorrow's world;
- to believe in your potential and in that of others, always;

---

1. Thierry Schneider was one of the speakers invited to this conference on 5 April 2002, with Bill Clinton, David Douillet, Robin S. Sharma and Tom Hopkins.

- to never give up knowing that perseverance is always preferable;
- not to be a slave to your emotions, but to be their master;
- to follow the life rhythm of your heart;
- to live your daily life with passion;
- to tap into your childhood soul by always encouraging the power of the imagination...

May you become this Athlete of Life who acts, his actions replacing his words...
This Athlete of Life who laughs and whose humor is his fountain of youth...
This Athlete of Life who loves, because loving is living!

THIERRY SCHNEIDER

PREFACE BY MIKE HORN

We each have our own way of living and find pleasure in doing things and using what we have that is unique to us.

Many people forget to make the most of the present moment, putting off their projects until tomorrow, forgetting that, tomorrow, it may be too late.

We live only once so why not go a little further? Why don't we push ourselves to explore new ground, try something new, get the most out of life? We are all capable of much, much more than we realize.

What is important, is to understand what makes us happy and to live for ourselves, not for others. Life comes from inside us, not from outside.

Read this inspiring book and become an Athlete of Life day after day... Only action will give you the opportunity to materialize your dreams!

"What we dream we can do."

"Obstacles are only as big as you want to make them!"

MIKE HORN
Professional Adventure

*"Thank you, Thierry, for everything you have done for me.
Why say: 'I can't', when I could say, 'I can'?"*

MIKE HORN

S ince the first edition of this book, Mike has accomplished new exploits. A few months ago, in March 2006, he set off from Russia, along with Norwegian explorer Borge Ousland, and reached the North Pole on foot, pulling a sledge 1,000 kilometers (621 miles), in complete darkness for sixty-one days and in temperatures nearing minus forty degrees.

From 2002 to 2004, he circumnavigated the Arctic circle, 20,000 kilometers (12,430 miles), solo and without the aid of any motorized transport or dogs. This expedition was called Arktos and began at the North Cape. Mike then crossed Greenland, the North of Canada, Alaska, the Bering Strait and Siberia, completing the adventure where it had started twenty-seven months earlier.

Mike Horn is also the first person in the world to successfully travel around the Earth along the Equator without motorized transport. He called this solo voyage of 40,000 kilometers (24,855 miles) and which took seventeen months, "Latitude Zero".

Who better than Mike Horn to personify the saying "Everything is possible", a credo that empowers all Athletes of Life?

www.mikehorn.com
Three books in Éditions XO
Latitude Zero, 25,000 miles around the equator
Conquering the impossible: My 12,000-Mile Journey
Around the Arctic Circle
Schooled by Far North

Part One

ATHLETE OF LIFE

INTRODUCTION

Act or Be Acted Upon?

E very day, we have a wonderful opportunity to confront the dilemma: act or be acted upon? For far too long, I believed that pressure was just a natural part of human life, something I had to endure with a certain amount of fatalism. But why not choose a different path, a path of wonderment? If we are fully aware that every moment we can reinvent our lives, create our ideal environment, live in harmony and good health, and enjoy generous and fulfilling relationships, we can reach a higher ground.

My coaching background and my experience as a constantly evolving individual have gradually taught me that "pressure" doesn't really exist. It is just the product of a mental state, reacting to an external environment. In fact, pressure results from a misperception of a given situation experienced at a given moment. What counts is not what happened, but how I perceive it and react to it. Failure to interpret an event correctly can lead to a disequilibrium.

Misperception can come from a variety of sources. But it usually arises from an assessment based on other people's opinions. Athletes for example, may be swayed by coaches, teammates, opponents, or the media. Business people may be influenced by stock holders, associates, consultants, or clients. Artists may be misled by directors, producers, agents, or critics. Students may be pressured by professors, examiners, parents, or other students. We are often affected by people in whom we place our undivided trust. It is a vicious circle. We constantly strive to prove ourselves, to please people who are supposedly wiser than we are. In so doing, we sabotage our potential. We lose our bearing, we no longer have our inner reference points. Constantly seeking reinforcement hither, thither and yon impedes healthy, inspiring performance.

Feeling alone against the entire world, we often seek reassurance from friends, family or associates. This is not at all unusual: we need confidence. It is an essential component of high performance. But the endless pursuit of approval can be habit forming. Unfortunately, we develop the habit of being acted upon. We surrender our autonomy and we perform well enough as long as we find support in our environment. But we are gnawed by a persistent fear that we will lose confidence. So left to our own devices, we unconsciously undermine our precious potential. We have failed to observe one fundamental principle of life: what I am seeking is already in me; no one can give me what I already own!

THE MAIN POINTS OF THIS INTRODUCTION

I invite you to put into practice, in your everyday life, the action principles that guide the Athlete of Life:

1) I know that what counts is not what happens but how I perceive it and react to it.

2) I am completely aware that "what I am seeking is already in me and no one can give me what I already own!". Therefore, I develop confidence in myself above all else.

3) My personal power lies in my capacity, at any time, to be able to create my life, whether it is my ideal environment, my vitality or fruitful and energizing relationships.

Chapter 1
THE POWER OF CONFIDENCE

The force to act

T rue confidence comes from within. Our essential task is to harness our energy to cultivate this vital resource. Everything begins within us! We can take a tip from Athletes of Life. For Athletes of Life, high performance is primarily an inward journey. They know that as long as they look outside themselves, they will lack the consistency that comes from self-mastery. Achievement is a question of attitude. And a winning attitude generates a winning temperament!

As we have seen, we have two choices: we can act or be acted upon.

The Reactive Athlete

When we are prisoners of fear, we see life as a constant struggle. Athletes are pitted against spectators, the field, the officials, the ball, the goal posts, the opponents and the wind. Business people battle with clients, managers, surprises, meetings, the agenda, statistics, computer and clock. Artists wrestle with critics, directors, other actors, lighting, the mike, and silence or restlessness in the theater. Whatever the activity, the environment is unconsciously seen as a set of destabilizing elements in which insecurity reigns.

In this fragile state, we are forced to strive to "survive," just to keep our spot on the team, our place in a business, our role in a play. We may resort to bluff and bravado to pretend we are supermen or superwomen, that we have everything under control.

But it's all an unconscious charade masking an overwhelming fear of rejection. When we are in this state, a feeling of separateness from the group is not uncommon. We are on the defensive; we're back on our heels; we resist. Even with the best will in the world, we can't commit ourselves 100% to our training, to our work, or to our role. Our sense of self seems to be slipping away. We are involved in a sort of pantomime.

Reactive Athletes suffer a similar fate. They spend a great deal of energy showing they are up to the task. They often overtrain. But it is a vicious circle. They make rapid progress, but they end up exhausted. They can engage in this gargantuan struggle over the short term, but in the long term it uses them up, chews them up, and spits them out. A series of counter performances may ensue accompanied by slight injuries followed by more serious ones, sickness, relational conflicts, doubts, even anguish and mounting panic. Clearly, these are outward manifestations of inner turmoil. Plagued by self doubt, they tend to exclude themselves from the group.

This chaos reflects a life that is out of whack. As the old adage goes, as we sow, so shall we reap. If we disregard the natural order of things, unfortunate consequences inevitably result. They have failed to keep their eye on the prize. Their self-esteem is at its lowest ebb. They suffer from a growing sense of insecurity. They go through the day with a negative and destructive attitude. In those dark moments, people become despondent and fall prey to some dependency. They need someone to lean on. All too often, the people around them may well respond by being judgmental. Just when they need someone to lend an ear, they encounter nothing but criticism.

The sad reality is that Reactive Athletes see their malaise reflected in their actions. If they don't get relief, they may exhaust themselves in counter-performance and even crash and burn like some young prodigies or type A managers. They are like shooting stars: here today and gone tomorrow.

In short, as long as we obsess about "proving" ourselves, we accept to be acted upon. We're on a downward spiral. Failure is practically inevitable. The phenomenon can be expressed by the following equation:

• Struggle against/division/resistance/doubt/fear = loss of energy, decline

So, don't wait until you suffer the slings and arrows of outrageous fortune before you decide to give your life real meaning.

The Path of the Creative Athlete

A fundamental lesson that Creative Athletes have to teach us is that we have absolutely nothing to prove to anyone. Quite simply, we *are*. Creative Athletes know their real power comes from inner strength, serenity in the face of inner demons. It is available to them in ample supply every day. They know why they have become an athlete, a business person, a sales rep, or an artist; they feel good about themselves, open and harmonious because they have chosen the life they lead. They embrace life! You can make no greater decision than to live your own life and to lead it from this precious moment on! You alone have the power to re-invent yourself.

Creative athletes don't need pep talks; they don't need cheerleaders. They keep their eye on their prize and work steadily to build their inner confidence on a firm foundation. In this regard, they realize that every situation is an opportunity for personal growth. Their unique goal is to continually develop the practice of *authentic perception*. Everything is in place to help them progress, evolve, and develop self-mastery. Athletes of Life have a positive impact on their own lives by dedicating themselves to their bold mission. Working from the inside to the outside: that is the sole objective of their daily endeavor. This is what I define as "mental, emotional and physical martial arts," everything aimed at proactivity.

Athletes of Life see *possibility* where others see adversity. They don't grouse and complain when something hasn't been done. They find a way to get it done "here and now." They have grasped a fundamental truth: they're not responsible for what others think of them. They can't get inside other people's heads. But, as Athletes of Life, they are responsible for what goes on inside their own head. That is where the potential lies. They build their own success working from the inside out. They take a page out of the martial arts, they don't struggle needlessly against the adversary or the environment. In sport, they are energized by spectators, field, officials, ball, goal posts, opponents, and wind. In business, they use the energy from clients, managers, surprises, meetings, the agenda, statistics, computer, and clock. And in theatre, they get the best out of critics, directors, other actors, lighting, the mike, and silence or restlessness in the theater. It is a strategy that works in any sector of activity.

Creative athletes know that everything is in place to accomplish their noble mission: the pursuit of excellence. This is the way it is going to be, because they have decided it! Hence, the extraordinary inner power of Athletes of Life. They have conquered their "demons of doubt." All around them, they find support to help them attain their objectives. They transform obstacles into allies. Thus they create an environment to maximize their own resources.

It is all a question of choice and perspective. The fans, officials, ball, goal posts, playing field, and weather can become an athlete's best friends. The same applies to referees, teammates, and coaches. In business, difficult clients, tight budgets, and bickering associates can be considered allies. A creative artist can take a complicated script, a cold audience, and a rickety old theater, and turn them into a play of vibrant characters in a dynamic, passionate adventure. Athletes of Life view opponents as ideal partners who enable them to find surprising solutions to new problems.

Like Antoine de Saint-Exupéry's *Little Prince*, they benefit from every situation that presents itself. Their attitudes and manner exude confidence. Whatever happens, they have the deep belief that whatever happens serves a noble cause. They understand the vital effect of muscle relaxation on performance: a tense body hampers performance. Confidence comes from within.

Letting go means that you have the courage to believe in what you can do. Your strength resides in your ability to discover, in every situation, an opportunity for greater self-mastery and creativity.

No matter the task, even amidst turmoil and confusion, Athletes of Life profoundly believe that they have no greater friend than life itself. The rest follows naturally: respect from their entourage, including their partners, customers, opponents, and the media. They become the cause, not the helpless plaything of *consequences*. They realize that to *understand*, they must act and that understanding brings wisdom.

They radiate, inspire, reassure. They embody the following action equation:
Work /unite/flexibility/confidence/enthusiasm = greater energy, belief

It is up to you to decide!

THE MAIN POINTS OF THIS CHAPTER

I invite you to put into practice, in your everyday life, the action principles that guide the Athlete of Life:

1) I am aware that optimum performance is, above all, the product of self-development.

2) I know that adopting the attitude of a champion will naturally give me a winner's temperament.

3) I develop the practice of authentic perception – everything is in place to help me progress, evolve and develop self-mastery.

4) I am responsible for what goes on inside my head and this is what I must master above all.

5) On the other hand, I am not responsible for what others think of me. Therefore, I have absolutely nothing to prove to anyone.

6) I consider myself as the cause of what happens to me and not a victim of the consequences of my actions. And I know that Life itself is my greatest friend!

Chapter 2
THE POWER OF BELIEF

The force to believe

We are all familiar with the saying "seeing is believing." But the converse is also true: *believing is seeing!* In short, as they used to say about the New York Mets, "You gotta believe!" Extraordinary performance starts with belief. It is the enormous power that Athletes of Life have at their disposal. As we have seen, everything begins with simple perceptions that depend entirely on us. We have free will. We can choose how we think, speak and act.

Too often, we fail to take advantage of our enormous capacity to effect change. We perpetuate habits that, at best, leave us in a position to endure life. When we are out of balance, we take it for our normal state. When something seems normal, we repeat it unconsciously without wondering whether it is really useful.

Scientists have found that human beings are bombarded by about 60,000 thoughts a day, 95% of which are leftovers from the previous day. If we don't find an effective way to process this information, we find ourselves in a chaotic and frustrating predicament. Remember: *our thoughts become our words, our words become our acts, our acts determine the results.*

A second revelation from Athletes of Life is that *above all, they create results*. They teach us to assume responsibility for our own creative process by building a solid foundation for future success. Everything depends on our attitude. If we aim to surpass our deepest expectations about what is possible, we can transform our lives.

Athletes of Life understand that to accomplish any worthwhile objective, they have to have a profound belief that they can do it. There's no point blaming circumstances, other people, or themselves. They consciously aim to reach a higher ground. If they are dissatisfied with their results, they decide to embark on the "natural process" that will lead them to success! They are no longer prisoners of appearances. They don't fear failure: they know failure is just part of the process.

Let's take a concrete example. A young woman is frustrated about her cigarette dependency. Cigarette ads promise her the moon. Smoking, they say, is a liberating experience. Yet, here she is, trapped behind a wall of smoke. Sure she's slim enough, and her best friend never tires of pointing it out. Of course, her nonsmoking friend is constantly griping about those extra pounds!

Now, the young woman has a couple of choices. One could result in profound personal failure: she could literally get stuck. But she could also decide that her habit of taking smoking breaks is not a failing; it is a situation she has deliberately created. The truth is, she has perfected a strategy for accomplishing her goal as a smoker. By reframing the situation, she can see herself not as "a failure," but as "a creator of results"!

And if the results don't suit her, she can devise a strategy to liberate herself from her dependency. She can use a natural process for her well-being instead of her ill-being. If she chooses to think, speak, and act differently about her "previous objective," the rest will follow naturally! Consciously motivated to change, the young woman, will be astonished to discover the advantages of being a smoker!

It is just a matter of changing her perspective. As a coach, I've tried this approach with my team of instructors a number of times.

The smoker is organized enough to take pauses, during which she finds herself, as often as not, connected to her inner self. She is deluded into thinking that cigarettes bring her the well-being she seeks. In fact, with each puff, she mobilizes her respiratory system: that is the real source of her relief! Amidst her torment, she is unconsciously practising the art of breathing.

And this point leads us to another important question! Why do smokers gain weight when they give up smoking? From a physiological standpoint, the lymphatic system helps eliminate toxins from the body. As a health and fitness instructor, I have observed that proper breathing reduces water retention, caused by a defective lymphatic system. To function, the circulatory system relies on the pumping of the heart, but the lymphatic system depends heavily on the respiratory mechanism.

When smokers break their habit, they put on weight because they no longer derive the same benefits from the process. And their mind tells them that they can compensate by eating more.

To sum up: the aim is not to encourage people to smoke, but to encourage them to see what is actually happening, and use what they learn! When she gives up cigarettes, the young woman can replace her smoking breaks with energy breaks entirely devoted to breathing. She can adopt the guilt-free practice immediately or progressively, depending on how she feels. For example, she can smoke cigarettes for enjoyment and eliminate the ones she smokes mechanically, do some deep breathing instead. Then, according to her personal rhythm and desire, she can gradually liberate herself from the yoke by improving her breathing mechanism.

Meanwhile, her friend has been practicing deep breathing, too. As a result, she has regained the svelte figure of her youth.

Athletes of Life are familiar with the saying "believing is seeing!" "You gotta believe!" Belief is the weapon of champions. It has nothing to do with a lack of humility. It has everything to do with the power of concentration applied to their daily tasks to realize their most ambitious vision.

Here's another illustration of the power of belief. A 29-year old salesman has been working in a multinational for a few months. The company has been undergoing a painful restructuring process. For the past ten years, he has worked in sales in two small family businesses. Though he had no formal professional training or diploma, and he was a little difficult to get along with, people thought he had potential. But his annual results, were less than spectacular. Even so, one day he happened to run into a former customer. The two of them had built a relationship of trust. The long and the short of it was he ended up applying for a sales job in a famous multinational. To his astonishment, he was offered a six-month contract on a trial basis.

Now, the young man could choose one of two "root beliefs": one debilitating; the other energizing!

He could consider the situation precarious and decide "here and now" to believe that:
- He's just another sales rep in the company; too boot he has been hired on trial;
- Layoff rumors are rampant, and that's all his associates talk about;
- His track record is hardly inspiring;
- He's had little gratification in his young career;
- He wasn't really offered the job; he got it through a contact; perhaps it was just a coincidence;
- The sales objectives are overly ambitious;

- Everyone knows that his sales area is really tough;
- He has a bad personality, as his father, teachers, and his last two bosses have repeatedly told him;
- His significant other has left him for someone else, conclusive proof that he is a mediocre, not to say hopeless person.

So, he could conclude that it would be foolish to hope for a productive, successful professional career—at least, that's exactly what he heard on the grapevine. He's not a bad salesperson, they say, but he's hardly a genius. His communications skills are acceptable, but unfortunately he's been catapulted into the position a little too late. He should be happy that he's got the job. It'll look good in his CV. But let's be serious: the best salespeople are in a different world.

And of course, he's right. You can see it in the way he thinks, the way he acts, the way he goes about things! Unconsciously, he's lugging around negative baggage from the past. The talk around the office is: "He's just not talented enough."

Nevertheless, he buckles down. He works hard, takes seminars, makes appointments, and visits clients. But he is dragging around a "limiting belief." It saps his strength of character, and his potential for spontaneous, instinctive action. He mutilates his "being" in the present moment. He's wracked by bitterness, frustration, doubt, and fear. He's a perfect illustration of what we mean by the reactive athlete on a "path of submission."

Try as he might, he can't put body and soul into his job. He is going through a sort of pantomime. Every morning, he trudges off to work with the weight of the world on his shoulders, shackled by negative opinions that seem to be swirling around him. What's worse, he is *unaware that he is unaware*. It's a horrible state for anyone to be in! He's so accustomed to the negativity, it seems completely normal. He repeats the same old patterns over and over, since he doesn't see any way out.

On the other hand, he could choose to act instead of being acted upon. He can decide to say, "Let the training begin!" And there is a fair bit of work to be done. He has to learn how to be a winner, how to be effective, how to become an Athlete of Life, fully *conscious* and spontaneous in each moment. This is where the coach intervenes. A true coach can make his charges aware when they are their own worst enemy! He can make them aware that they are unaware, that there is more to life than simply enduring.

Now, by choosing this path, our sales rep can reclaim his personal power. If, for example, he acts too impulsively, because of a feeling of insecurity, he can gradually liberate himself from this pattern of behavior.

His coach can help him discover the reason for his lack of success. Then he will see what caused his mistakes. Soon, he will be aware of his mistakes while he is making them, and in the end he can avoid them.

That's how Athletes of Life—be they pianists, skiers, dancers, businesspersons, teachers, or retired people—function all the time. They think, speak, and act effectively, at the right time and the right place.

Let's return to our little story. The same salesman with the same potential, the same experience and in the same environment can choose to act on an energizing "root belief." What if he perceives the situation in a different light? It's an excellent opportunity. Things aren't so bad. He does have a job with a multinational, albeit for a trial period even though he has never been known for his professional skills! Deep down, he knows that his atypical career path reflects his uniqueness. He was lucky enough not to tread the beaten trail, so he has developed his individuality.

He is perfectly aware of what they say about him: he's already gone pretty far, let's be serious, they say. "Top-level sales is another matter entirely. Getting sales out of his client sector is like drawing blood from a stone, even for experienced salespersons." He's boiling inside; he is in an intense vibratory state! His senses are pulsating with energy; his heart, his self-esteem are urging him on:

"Accept the challenge, be thankful that this is the way they see you here and now: they're offering you a powerful action lever! Sure, you don't have much experience compared with the top sales reps, but you have a dream, a vision: to radiate from every pore in your body the need to serve Life. Deep down inside, you have understood Colin Turner's words: According to Colin Turner, when you're going through the motions of "work," you're just doing or producing something. But when you're providing "service," you *become* someone! Never forget that delivering better-than-excellent "service" doesn't mean merely doing the client a favor. It's a way of life.

As Hermann Hesse wrote, "He who wishes to live long must serve, but he who wishes to rule does not live long." So, invest your energy in the fundamental human values that you always believed in. They may have earned you the reputation of being quite a character! But it's precisely because of that character that you believe everything is possible! You are "in the right place at the right time." The greatest salespeople, like the greatest athletes and artists are people who believed in themselves, when no one else had faith in them, which is the mark of a true champion!

Colin Turner is right! Yes, he is empowered by the "root belief" that energizes Athletes of Life: "Everything is possible!" *Their thoughts show it, their words show it, their daily acts show it.* They have chosen to rise above the debilitating conditions of their past and use them as a springboard for their hidden inner resources.

They know they have their own particular talent and they strive to develop it meticulously, day after day, at work and in other activities. They work, visit clients, attend seminars and company meetings. In all their endeavors, they are buoyed by the exhilarating belief that "Everything is possible." It puts steel in their character; it empowers them to act instinctively and spontaneously. They speak from the gut, fill the present moment with their authentic being, and create a state of enthusiasm, exaltation, happiness, flexibility, and efficiency. They have a core belief that inventors, adventurers, and champions—the celebrities who have marked their era—succeeded because they were unreasonable. They pushed on, in the firm belief that they would realize their dreams! They took the "path of action," of creativity, the royal road travelled by Athletes of Life. Deep down inside, they knew that *energy was wherever they brought their attention to bear.*

As we have seen, when we dream big, we can make it happen! There's just as much reason to believe that we will attain our objective as to believe that we won't. So, we need to find a way to achieve our mission, to mobilize our strength in order to trigger an action that will bring us closer to our final goal, instead of inventing a million and one reasons why our dream is impossible.

Unconsciously, ordinary athletes poison themselves with "limiting beliefs." They know they will never really excel. It's a self-fulfilling prophesy. They believe they will fail and they constantly ruin any possibility of success.

Athletes of Life, make a conscious choice to realize their "energizing beliefs." They think they are capable; therefore they are. They believe in the possibility of success and constantly prepare the path to achieve it.

It's up to you to decide!

THE MAIN POINTS OF THIS CHAPTER

I invite you to put into practice, in your everyday life, the action principles that guide the Athlete of Life:

1) I know that above all in order to be able to *visualize* the achievement of my goals I have to *believe in them*.

2) I have understood that the feeling of imbalance has imposed itself upon me as a "normal state". Therefore, I am going to repeat it unconsciously, without ever questioning its usefulness... and therefore imprison myself further in this *imbalance*.

3) I am above all a "creator of results":
   my thoughts become my words, my words are transformed into actions, my actions determine results. I therefore have the ability to put in place a "winning strategy", by taking care to think, speak and act differently when the result that I have brought about does not satisfy me or no longer satisfies me.

4) I bring a creative response to all situations I come across, rather than wallowing in the role of the victim, who always blames the circumstances, other people or spitefully blames himself.

5) As an Athlete of Life, my motivation is to *get out of the habit* of not acting like a winner. To do this, I assimilate the four learning phases, namely that:

   – I am unaware that I am unaware;
   – I become aware that I am unaware;

– I become aware that I am aware;
– I become unaware that I am unaware.

This means that I think, speak and act effectively at the right time and in the right place.

6) I use this key principle of the Athlete of Life, according to which energy is wherever I bring my attention to bear. What I expect is always possible – therefore, if I feel capable of achieving my goal, I become it, and I am going to prepare the path to achieve it. I dare to be "unreasonable", believing above all in my capacity to realize my dreams, even if no one yet has confidence in me.

7) I have understood that service enables me to "become someone", whereas the concept of work can only "produce something"…

Chapter 3
THE POWER OF FREE WILL

The force to decide

C learly "not choosing is a choice." Of course, Athletes of Life are human. Like the rest of us, they do make decisions in many different situations. All too often, we make our decisions out of habit. Unfortunately, there is no serious training program to teach us how to improve our decision-making skills. Bear in mind that there is every reason to believe that the decisions we make now will determine our future.

Too frequently, as we have seen, we react to a situation by some unconscious reflex. We resort to responses that gave us comfort in the past though they are completely inappropriate to the problem at hand. Endlessly recycling our behaviour, we create a vast debilitating pattern that we call stress.

In one of my previous works *Coeur à Coeur*,[1] I used an analogy about chocolate cake to explain the damaging mechanism of habits and their harmful consequences if they are not used for our well-being. It goes as follows: You're battling the bulge, but you have a sweet tooth for chocolate. One day, you walk by your favorite pastry shop, and in the window is a chocolate mousse cake! You are sorely tempted. Your taste buds rule. Just a piece can't do any harm. You enter the shop as if in a trance. Back outside, you quickly down the tender morsel before going back to work as if nothing has happened. The story illustrates the three stages of habits:

---

1.   Published by Éditions Un monde différent.

41

1. First, the sudden appearance of desire at the mere sight of chocolate cake. An external event occurs right before your eyes and the mechanism is triggered. You fall under the spell of the treat.
2. Then, the anticipated pleasure spurs you to action, and you buy the cake.
3   Finally you eat it, reinforcing the memory of how much you enjoy chocolate cake, but also intensifying your feeling of guilt!

So it is an unconscious process. It applies to all your habits, whether they facilitate or impede your development. To leave the "path of submission," Athletes of Life liberate themselves from the fear of the unknown. They know the emotion is anathema to change, evolution and success. According to Rainer Maria Rilke, "We cannot create the future by dredging up memories of the past. To believe we can is to be misled by fear born from this misconception." Hence it is vital that you become as *conscious* as possible in your everyday life.

Above all, Athletes of Life accept themselves. They accept what the choices or "non-choices" they made in the past have made them. They know that their thoughts and feelings are not there to dictate to them, but to serve them. If they are not content with their past decisions or the present situation—no matter what life brings them—they can always make another *decision,* "here and now." Every time they respond creatively to a given situation, they become stronger.

Most people bitterly attribute setbacks to other people, circumstances, or their own "worthlessness." But Athletes of Life enjoy making decisions. They assume success in advance. In this state of mind, these champions feel free to decide who they are, how they live, and what they will accomplish. They are free of constraints because they have made their own choices: being true and authentic allows them to create and be created!

They don't rehash the past. They don't bathe in self-criticism about what they have done or not done. They look ahead to find solutions. Personal responsibility has forever become their home ground and with it they gain real power over their future. Since they can always end relationships, they are, paradoxically, more comfortable about getting involved in them. Day after day, they train how to say "no." So they can say "yes" to life and to its myriad opportunities.

Athletes of Life have discovered the power of their "inner axis." Step by step, they tap into their own inner resources instead of borrowing strength from other people. At every moment of the day, their consciousness can illuminate the "real solution." To be conscious means to refuse to engage in inner polemics with saboteurs such as doubt, fear, jealousy, hatred and panic. These feelings prevent us from experiencing happiness in the here and now.

True inner security allows Athletes of Life to successfully meet their challenges and to do so with gusto. Their deeply rooted strength represents their invulnerability, the formidable weapon that they never surrender. They use every moment of their lives to train consciously to regain the power of free will. With this incredible instrument, they gradually build a springboard to success. Their goal is certainly not to defend their arguments tooth and nail. On the contrary, they attempt to make the most noble decisions that will bring them closer to their ultimate objective: self-mastery. When they achieve that, they are in possession of an art that can deal with any situation. They are not reduced to enduring the game of life. They continually radiate confidence from within.

They are vigilant, but serene, like a cat ready to pounce when the opportunity presents itself.

Let's look at a concrete example from tennis.

In competition, Athletes of Life pulsate with power. They act; their opponents are the ones who are acted upon. Their very presence makes their adversaries less spontaneous, less in touch with the rhythm of the match because they are forced to think about their game. Thinking makes them hesitate and, as the adage goes, he or she who hesitates is lost.

In fact, players are thrown off their game when they ask themselves "should I hit the ball right or left? Should I hit cross-court or smash?" because they are looking for the ideal play. More often than not, the result is an error, a pitiful attempt that goes awry because it was governed by the fear of making a mistake. Athletes of Life, on the other hand, don't give in. They don't give their adversary any option. Quite simply, they are completely present in the situation, sure of themselves, rooted in inner confidence. Thus they can be spontaneous. They don't try to impress their adversaries. They are masters of the court; they are in the zone. Udoubtedly, they *are* open to the magic of the moment. They radiate a confidence that tells their opponent: "I have everything to win!" A message that their opponent translates by "I have everything to lose."

How often have we seen players botch a perfectly easy ball and fall awkwardly because they overhit their backhand by waiting too long or by rushing and squandering a splendid opportunity? It happens all the time. How many athletes have lost decisive points in a match through a lack of inner vigilance? However, rarely do we hear the TV commentator say that the other player's overwhelming presence reversed the formula: submit-act into act-make submit.

I perceive action to be the expression of an internal state of being, a feeling of certainty, consciously chosen by the Athlete of Life. Their adversary is acted upon and made to react. I often see, even at the highest level, no matter what the sport, most athletes—who physically and technically are extraordinary—broken down mentally. They allow themselves to submit to their own adversities: letting themselves be disturbed by the weather, the reaction of their fans, aggressive comments in the media, the charisma of their opponents or the comments and doubts, even unexpressed, of their own coach. "Silly injuries" crop up supposedly at the worst possible moment. Of course, you can easily apply this example to your own life: the only way you can unlearn your personal shortcomings is to spend time observing how you deal with situations in your daily life.

Further on in the book, we will examine in greater detail the vital influence of physiology, posture, and movement on whether or not we or the people around us make decisions. If we don't act on our environment, it will act on us, whether we like it or not. According to the universal laws of life, by changing our choices and decisions, we give ourselves a chance to grow, supported by our environment. Athletes of Life no longer consider opponents people who are ready to make their lives miserable, but allies, partners, and teachers along the way who give them a opportunity to display their skills. It's their choice! So, they respect their opponents as much as they respect themselves and they are thankful that they encounter their adversaries because in doing so they have to face themselves, their limitations, and their inner demons.

In the arena, in the office or on stage, if we lose our support, literally or figuratively, we can do no better than to endure our existence. Whatever the events going on around us, we can decide what to do. Athletes of Life know that, as long as their senses are clouded by stress, they will be hostage to false issues: how can I seek creative solutions when I'm wracked by doubt and confusion? The only liberating question is to know how to eliminate anguish so that I can "live big," live my dream, with a liberated, limpid and clear spirit? And the wise response is always found in the deepest part of them: "do I feel an expansion or a contraction?" This simple question already answers the question "What do I do?"

It bears repeating: nothing good can come from an inner state that is under stress! The only fit practice for an Athlete of Life is to develop step by step the capacity to remain calm in all circumstances. If we find ourselves gripped by fear, we eliminate this state of malaise as quickly as possible using the power of exhalation and benefiting from the mastery of our breathing mechanism. It is so simple and obvious that in no field of activity do people take the time to concentrate on this essential age old training technique! To do it, we have to discard an old mask that is so easy to wear: that of the victim!

An example from my personal experience may help illustrate the point. Some time ago, I was a soccer goalkeeper. Like so many other things, my sports career left a lasting impression on me, unconsciously of course, like so many others. Often I found my-self out of sync. Like the tennis players I just mentioned, I was being acted upon more than I was acting. I suffered from an inner imbalance, I had lost my inner frame of reference, lost my points of support, both literally and figuratively. In fact, I would stumble backwards—further demonstration of the disarray that caused me to submit to the event. I found that the state of mind between the goal posts was poisoned by a false belief. Everything is a matter of belief; so we have discovered. And what's worse the most paralyzing block that a goalkeeper experiences is that every soccer player, coach and goalkeeper, unconsciously associates the plight of "victim" to this marvelous position of last defense. This has become the most misleading image that a goalkeeper suffers. A player who is so different from the others, not only because he wears another jersey: when an attacker gets a breakaway on him, everyone sees the predator that is going to devour its prey. All the goalkeeper can do is to run out helplessly toward the attacker to be subjected to the final attack, figuratively to be executed. The attacker's energizing belief is reinforced and the goalkeeper's limiting belief that he or she is a victim is strengthened. But what happens when the defender of last resort has sufficient strength of character to reverse the paradigm. The image of a goalkeeper "standing alone to face the entire world," has been of enormous benefit to me in my life. It helped me meet challenges with the insouciance and aplomb of a child. Whether it is the result of the rejection of a professional project, faced with the "risk" of meeting, in the street, the wonderful woman who might someday become the woman in my life— providing I make the first step to approach her—to go after a client "out of reach"; because I need to find a sum of money within 48 hours, to sell my product abroad before I could become a prophet in my own land, to teach some exercises widely performed all over the planet after being the laughing stock among dance professionals, to dance and sing in front of a large audience, with no particular predisposition, to write one and even several books despite a singularly undistinguished academic career, to stretch morning after morning, year after year until I could finally do the splits though my former coaches told me I wasn't naturally supple; whether it involves speaking in front of large audiences even though I had been extremely shy when I sat with more than six people at the table, to believe in my physical capacities which were said to be limited.

Yes, I was on my own in goal. I had learned to stand tall and pursue my dream. It was then or never. Mike Horn is the epitome of a true Athlete of Life. He was the first person to complete a solo trip, circumnavigating the world by land and by sea, along the equator. The voyage took 17 months and covered 40,000 kilometers (25,000 miles) below latitude 0. He would often tell me with a big smile, "The impossible is just what man has not yet made possible." What a wonderful idea!

Think of how two boxers, wrestlers, or judokas face off before a match. Think of the determination in trapeze artists' eyes before they risk their lives, performing without a net because it is their choice, fully responsible. The intensity of their look shows the power of the rootedness, the capacity for confidence of all athletes that their bodies radiate around them, the well-known "presence" or charisma.

The Athletes of Life always decide to shape, to build their inner self first, to proceed to the external. They are constantly re-inventing their lives. They don't lie awake at night, wondering whether they are in the right job, in the right house, or with the right spouse.

They are fully aware that they can choose between two distinct paths: they can choose to be happy and fulfilled, providing things turn out the way they want, or they can resolve to be happy and fulfilled whatever the results of their decisions. And they know that the second option gives them more control over their lives. Athletes of Life immediately *become* their dream because they have discovered that decision-making is not a matter of words; it is a matter of action. Life is wonderful, generous. For them, it is a marvelous game because they have chosen it. Others see it as a stubborn struggle, an endless combat, obligations, a prison...

It is up to you to decide!

THE MAIN POINTS OF THIS CHAPTER

I invite you to put into practice, in your everyday life, the action principles that guide the Athlete of Life:

1) I know deep down that *not choosing is a choice...*

2) I have perfectly assimilated the unconscious mechanism of habit. An event occurs and the mechanism is triggered, I submit to it:
   – desire incites me to act;
   – I act based on habit;
   – my action reinforces the previous memory.

3) My goal is to become always more conscious, in my everyday life, so as not to repeat my inappropriate behavior. The real solution is always where my awareness is focused. It is up to me to learn how to manage it based on what I want, rather than on what I do not want, and especially not on what others want for me... I train myself to make the noblest choice that will optimize my self-mastery. My feelings are not there to lead me blindly but to serve me. The only question that can free me from stress, is how to eliminate my inner turmoil, to naturally find a clear and lucid spirit.

4) I accept that I am where I am because of my past choices or "non-choices". And if I am not satisfied with my current situation, I have the opportunity to make a different choice, here and now. I do not look back to criticize what I have or have not done, I find solutions. Each time I bring a creative response, I become stronger. By being true to myself I allow myself to create. To create myself! I give myself the freedom

to choose who I am, where I live and what I am going to accomplish.

5) I dare to commit myself fully to my relationships, because I know that I can choose to end them at any time. I am free. This is why I train myself to be able to say no, so that I can say yes to life without any reservations, when I become involved with others.

6) I make decisions by my actions and not by my words. I choose to be happy, whatever the results created by my decisions, and not only if things turn out as I want.

7) I have assimilated the fact that the intensity of my look reveals the power of my inner axis. This well-known "presence", this natural charisma, is born from the capacity for confidence that my body radiates around me.

Chapter 4
THE POWER OF THE PRESENT MOMENT

The force of attentiveness

Every moment is a new moment.
Every moment is a creative moment.
Every moment becomes a result.

As we have seen, we can be obsessed about doing everything perfectly or pleasing everybody. In that conflicted state of mind, we become tense, we lose our spontaneity and therefore, our ability to adapt. One of the most powerful assets Athletes of Life can develop is the capacity to be "present in every moment." In that heighten state of attentiveness, they become the "ideal action." They are no longer desperately trying to find out how to do it. And to radiate this "presence," we must be present now or never. The "here and now" becomes our anchor, the source of our success, our permanent training ground, our faithful ally. And to be in the *present moment* in the arena, on stage, or at the office, Athletes of Life systematically train themselves to "be" completely dedicated to all their daily tasks.

Athletes who cannot concentrate outside the arena cannot perform at their best. Indeed, if when they drive their little daughter to school, they're thinking of what their coach said, when they're having lunch with their spouse they're thinking about the next track meet, when they're driving their car, they're thinking about the lack of communication between them and their spouse, when they're brushing their teeth, they're thinking about an article in the paper, they have obviously failed to reach an advanced state of attentiveness, that ability to merge with the *present moment* to achieve success. Just the opposite, they are being acted upon by circumstances. And quite logically, under the intense conditions of competition, they inevitably become the plaything of events!

Athletes of Life know that it is vitally important to use every moment in the day to cultivate this state of "being." They know that it is crucial to focus on *being* rather than stubbornly trying to *do* a thing. They follow the natural order of *being, doing, and having,* instead of *having so that they can dare to do and eventually be.* As long as they "are," they naturally become the thought, word or deed that befits the situation, because they "are" the moment. To be focused, to "be" the *present moment* during a match, a sale, or a show, they learn to be just as attentive when they are brushing their teeth, tying their shoes, chatting with their daughter, or driving their car, as they are when they skillfully take the ball away from an opponent, clinch a sale, or stir the audience.

Deep down, Athletes of Life understand that the present moment is the right time, that this is the right place. They are in touch with their feelings because their body is always in the here and now. They have no choice. They can live only in the present moment! That is why they are mindful of their attitudes. They don't get endlessly bogged down regretting or ruing the past, or worrying about the uncertain, chimerical future. To persist, anguish and worry must be fed by the mind with images, internal dialogues, and unpleasant sensations that destroy the pristine purity of the moment. For anguish and worry to exist, they must be fed! Problems need attention to persist.

Instead of being shackled by bad habits, Athletes of Life undergo extensive mental training. They nurture their mind. They concentrate on what is happening here and now. They focus on achieving their objectives. Their state of mind is such that they can make use of everything to attain their dream. The energy is wherever they bring their attention to bear. So, they are attentive, they remain open and receptive to how their body feels. Their body constantly gives them all the information they need to maximize their potential. Concentration goes hand in hand with inner calm, so they cultivate fluidness of their breathing, which is a barometer of their presence in the moment.

Athletes of Life no longer classify things as important or as insignificant. They bring the same degree of dedication to every activity they engage in. This is their greatest asset. This is what is referred to as "satori," an optimal state of being that has *become their activity*, mentally, emotionally, and physically. Whatever their field of activity, they know that success primarily involves *being totally present in the moment*. If they play tennis, they know that victory or defeat depends on what they think about between points. Ordinary athletes waste precious time thinking about the ball they hit out, cursing out the line judge for a bad call, blaming themselves for missing out on a chance to gain the upper hand. As an Athlete of Life, you can focus on the quality of your exhalation, here and now. You can easily feel when you are breathing properly.

Driving to still another appointment, ordinary salespeople agonize. reciting the mantra that sales figures are all that counts, and that the next visit, as difficult as it may be, will determine their future. They impatiently smoke another cigarette, endure the heavy traffic, and frantically punch out numbers on their cellular, in a vain quest for relief. On the other hand, Sales persons who are Athletes of Life concentrate on the quality of their out-breath, here and now, focusing their entire being on those blissful moments of solitude, with their heart at ease.

Concentration goes hand in hand with the here and now.

In every moment, Athletes of Life *practice* their lives.

They are present in what they are doing, whatever the activity.

They become the action or movement.

They are the present moment.

They are quite simply the power of the here and now; they are pure creativity.

In fact, full consciousness reflects their true nature. All around them their presence embodies the art of living. They serenely build their future, step by step, moment by moment. They live one day at a time. They have become the path of happiness.

It's up to you to decide!

THE MAIN POINTS OF THIS CHAPTER

I invite you to put into practice, in your everyday life, the action principles that guide the Athlete of Life:

1) As an Athlete of Life, I have assimilated the fact that every moment is a new moment, every moment is therefore a creative moment and every moment naturally becomes a result!

2) By knowing how to be *present* in what I am living, I welcome this *present* that life offers me, *Presence!* Now is always the right moment, here is always the right place!

3) I know that above all I must concentrate on *being* rather than *doing*. The natural order is *being, doing, having* and not *having* in order to dare to do and eventually be.

4) Concentration goes hand in hand with inner calm, so I cultivate the flow of my breathing, which is a barometer of my presence in the moment.

5) Danger comes from incorrect use of my mind. If I do not control it, it can cast me into regrets of the past or fears for the future... For anguish and worry to exist, they must be fed. I cultivate my personal power knowing that, without attention, it is impossible for a problem to persist.

6) I choose to leave the limited territory where we classify things as important or insignificant. I engage in each of my activities with the same degree of dedication.

7) Success is above all a question of *presence* in the moment. I am present in what I do, I *have become* the movement, the words..., the right moment.

Chapter 5
THE POWER OF VISUALIZATION
The force of images

I t is extremely important for Athletes of Life to develop self-mastery. It is essential to develop the fundamental quality of pure attention, which is better known as concentration.

"The energy is wherever I bring my attention to bear." That is the revelation that guides Athletes of Life in their daily lives. Too often, the extraordinary capacities of the imagination, a fundamental faculty of the brain's right hemisphere, are not put to good use. We are prone—it's much easier—to concoct dark, fearsome narratives, rather than consciously using the power of our imagination in a constructive manner. Certainly, I can be acted upon by these misleading scenarios that I have inherited from my past. I can continue to be subjected to their devastating effects like a submissive victim or I can reclaim the power of my brain, here and now, and use its faculties to promote my own happiness.

Using the power of visualization and imagery, Athletes of Life systematically improve their behavior and performance. By controlling their mind, they affect their immediate environment. Energy always follows thought. It has been shown that imagined and real experiences have similar effects on our autonomic nervous system! As we have already seen, our perception of a situation will determine the way we interact with it through our thoughts, words, and deeds. In other words, we must *act* or *be acted upon*!

We don't react to reality as much as we react to our *image* of reality! Clearly, if our self-image is distorted, our response to situations we encounter will be inappropriate, and consequently our already debilitating lack of confidence will be reinforced.

Athletes of Life consciously decide to create positive, constructive images to gain control over their everyday life. They visualize themselves in a situation that offers new potential for expression. It is important to point out that we must "feel in the gut" the desired situation, that is see it, hear it, and feel it resonate in our flesh, to create "muscle memory," which will result in the perfect act in actual practice!

For the athlete, this type of training can be effective for developing technical, tactical, physical or emotional skills. For businesspeople the training is effective in communications, leadership, empathy, sales stress management and preventive health. For artists, it is useful for physical skills, concentration, sharing, sensitization, listening, action, and rhythm. You can gradually plan your own visualization strategy to complement your everyday work. But regular practice is essential. The results will be extraordinary! Athletes of Life know from personal experience that they are "unbeatable in their head," that "everything is possible in there," and that their autonomic nervous system registers the entire practice—each perfect act—creating a bodily memory that generates success.

Goalkeepers can easily visualize stopping 50 penalty stops. Trying to perform the same feat in real games is a bit more daunting. But why not act instead of being acted upon? True goalkeepers, Athletes of Life, have chosen to visualize a "successful save." By the time they face the shooter, they have already registered thousands of successful saves in their nervous system! So they are calm, confident, even serene and therefore effective.

The same holds true for golfers, skiers, gymnasts and other competitors. Sinking 50 putts in a row and performing perfectly on the green is certainly possible mentally, here and now. The rest will follow. Tearing down the hills at Innsbruck, Austria, visualizing and rehearsing the performance in detail on your bed in Calgary well before the competition is possible! Performing an innovative, spectacular routine on the rings and doing it successfully every time, feeling each of your muscles at work is also possible!

Succeeding in all your sales, even supposedly impossible ones, can be done in your head and can be felt in your body! And by the time you visit a client, you will already have closed the sale a hundred times. So you'll feel relaxed in the situation which you had previously visualized. In your mind, you have already spoken to the person and found out what he needed... and the rest follows naturally! If you are scheduled to perform at Théâtre Saint-Denis in Montreal or the Olympia in Paris, you can successfully and passionately rehearse the show many times. This will greatly enhance your chances of pulling off the performance that you had hoped to do.

It is very important to do some physical relaxation before engaging in a session of visualization. To be creative, open, and fertile, we must be in a state of inner peace. And as we will discover, the principle asset of Athletes of Life is a state of calm.

As far as Athletes of Life are concerned, training never ends! They realize that in order to change their reality—their existence—they can change their attitude, their behaviour and their perceptions. This is their masterpiece!

It is up to you to decide!

THE MAIN POINTS OF THIS CHAPTER

I invite you to put into practice, in your everyday life, the action principles that guide the Athlete of Life:

1) I use the power of imagery and the mastery of visualization to dedicate myself to improving my behavior, as well as my performance, by acting on my inner mind. By doing this I am indirectly able to affect my immediate environment.

2) I have learnt that an imaginary experience has the same effect on my autonomic nervous system as a real experience. And it is much easier for me to make x successful attempts of any activity *in my head*, than in real conditions...

3) I know that I never react to reality as much as to the image that I create of reality. Therefore, I put this capacity to its best possible use by creating the scenario the best adapted to my success.

4) As long as my self-image is distorted, my response to situations encountered can only be inappropriate, reinforcing my lack of self-confidence and, consequently, reducing my chances of success.

5) To gain control over my everyday life, I choose to create positive and constructive images.

6) It is essential that I "feel in the gut" the desired situation in order to create this "muscle memory", which will provide me, in actual practice, with the perfect act, the perfect situation...

7) I cultivate a state of inner peace, calm and relaxation to be as creative, open and fertile as possible.

Chapter 6
THE POWER OF EMOTION

The force of enthusiasm

Athletes of Life dare to live, to understand, to master their emotions. Etymologically, the word *emotion* means "stir up," "remove," "displace." Emotions are the most precious energy assets you have. Regardless of the activity, you must radiate enthusiasm, access a state of exaltation in order to excel. You are the only one who can cultivate the motivation, the essential ingredient for achieving any worthwhile goal. In this state of exaltation, the energy flows freely through your body, ready to ignite every gesture, every word, and every thought.

As we have seen, the fundamental goal of coaches, managers, and directors is to enable their protégés to constantly, consciously, take a path full of enthusiasm, exhilaration, and exaltation. When we are true to ourselves, we can be true leaders. We exude enthusiasm, inspiring people around us to accomplish their task and serve their community in their own way. Above all, leadership is taught by example. And, to have the privilege of leading others to fully invest in a cause, we must be fired with the determination to use our emotional energy for passion, not fear.

Passion is the seed of success. Athletes of Life grasp this fundamental truth. They manage their emotions harmoniously by constantly practising a "martial art" of the emotions, emotional Aikido. Sadness, fear, and anger impede success. So, they learn to recognize these emotions and accept them instead of resisting them, to understand and embrace them. Far from rejecting them, they take advantage of them!

In fact, Athletes of Life no longer think of these strong feelings as negative emotions: they know there is no deadlier poison than judgment. Their flights of anger, sadness, and fear—an amalgam of unpleasant emotions—teach them how to be true to themselves, to be authentic, to tune into what they really are: Athletes of Life! They are modern alchemists: they convert the heaviness, the weight, the emotional coagulation that imprisons the flesh and clouds the mind into fluid energy that releases their creativity. Only by constant daily practice, can they sublimate automatic, destructive behaviors. Then, pleasant emotions like joy, exaltation, enthusiasm, jubilation, and love will become performance's most faithful allies!

So, it is critically important to know why we experience pleasant and unpleasant emotions. What makes us act or react the way we do? Why is our body open or closed? In fact, there is a close correlation between our emotional state and our vital needs. To be in good health, we need to know how to respect who we really are. To do this, we train boldly to satisfy our needs, we learn how to position ourselves, to be true to ourselves, to be conscious, so that our identity, our security, our needs, and our integrity will be respected. Then, our emotional energy will flow freely, and we can maximize our performance.

Otherwise, we would be ignoring our essential human needs. We would plunge into a state of total insecurity and be blocked emotionally. Our capacity for self-expression would be seriously compromised. What's more, failure to take into account our emotional needs would destroy our self-esteem, make us even more bitter, and sap our energy.

Aware of this, Athletes of Life know that their emotions are "friendly signposts" along the path of life. It is essential to heed them. Emotions keep them constantly informed about whether they are respecting their vital needs, the compost of their authenticity, the precious secret inner garden they must protect from harmful intrusion. In the past, they sometimes caught themselves saying "yes" when in their gut, they wanted to say "no." But they were afraid to assert themselves, to reveal who they really were. They were too eager to please or they were looking for ego gratification, to make sure that people thought well of them. They lied to themselves to have a false sense of security.

Expanding or contracting? Their body constantly updates Athletes of Life about their emotional state. Its sole mission is to determine whether they are truly respecting themselves in every situation they encounter. Every malaise is the result of relational insincerity, which puts pleasing others above personal integrity. Society interprets completely natural qualities such as sensitivity and vulnerability as signs of weakness. Consequently, it imposes a rigid, mechanistic social code that insists that we suppress our emotions. This mistaken way of behaving is especially prevalent in the professional milieu, be it in business or sport, in which there is a constant effort to motivate individuals, on the one hand, and a continual attempt to prevent them from being themselves, on the other.

People are amalgams of emotions, guts, feelings, and pleasure. But all too often, they are turned into social puppets, expressing displeasure, frustration and inflexibility. When you water your garden, it is better if the water flows freely through the garden hose. In fact, if there are areas of resistance, even if the water flows normally into the hose, only a few drops of water will emerge at the other end. The result: frustration and aridness. Emotions are governed by the same principle. The natural order of things cannot be ignored: whether you like it or not, resistance to what is true produces unpleasant consequences.

And if you have failed so far to make healthy emotional management an integral part of your existence, it is high time that you do so, "here and now." Otherwise, every day your emotional immaturity will weigh down your body with suppressed emotional wastes that pollute your mind. Nature has given you this capacity; if you fail to use it wisely for your own good, unconsciousness will inevitably be your downfall. Again, you are free to choose: either you take full advantage of the power of your emotions or you become emotionally constipated, destroy your vitality, and get bogged down in frustration.

Tuning into yourself, being aware of who you really are, here and now, rather than stubbornly spending your time and energy at all costs! If you feel blocked, it is far more intelligent and constructive to acknowledge the resistance, accept it, seek out the cause, admit that it exists, since it does exist, and focus your energy on reestablishing a normal flow before undertaking any other action.

That is precisely what Athletes of Life are dedicated to doing. They nurture their emotional intelligence, while most of their opponents repeatedly resist events. They bitterly refuse to be themselves, preferring to conform to some image of strength and control. Athletes of Life literally breathe coherent thoughts, words and deeds. That's why they make great champions, great sales representatives, great artists, natural leaders who believe in what is true, no matter what happens. They constantly assume their responsibilities.

When they are angry or afraid, they don't lie to themselves. They don't deny the feeling, they don't resist it. They experience it consciously. They embrace it. They substitute softness for hardness, rigidity, and bitterness. They don't close up; they have the courage to open up to what they are feeling, to what they *are* here and now. They find another way, they boldly undo the tangled web that had ensnared them. Thus they have greater freedom. Their whole being surrenders once more to the freedom of expression they had as small children. They are no longer prisoners of misconceptions about the life they are leading. On the contrary, they live life to the full, with their whole being! They don't wrestle with life's hurdles. They treat them as friends. They even welcome their own negative reactions. They no longer block their vital energy; they can use "what is," so they can pursue their personal development.

As a rule, martial artists are taught not to react, but to respond. As in the practice of martial arts, which are inspired by the universal laws that govern life, when martial artists are pushed in one direction, they don't react by pushing in the opposite direction, they pull in the same direction, using the opponent's momentum to achieve success instead of wasting their energy resisting, fighting what is, making it bend to their will and to their limited view of the situation. Blood must circulate freely in our arteries, in order to ensure our health, and not coagulate, blocking and destroying its own mission. Similarly, we must flow freely and take the path of non-resistance in every circumstance in our lives. This is the best way to use our emotions and the extraordinary possibilities that they put at our disposal to keep going in the right direction, to benefit from the natural process of success or failure. It is up to us to choose, because whether we like it or not, it operates very much like the universal law of mass or gravity.

Athletes of Life practice the art of letting go. It allows them to gain control over their lives. The emotions are there to serve them; Athletes of Life understand the fundamental relationship between the emotions and the body. They are in touch with their bodies. When we suppress our emotions, ignore them, and reject them, we plunge a little deeper everyday into the mutilating process of passivity. Often, we prefer to remain in its grip because, despite the suffering we undergo, we feel reassured, because we are in familiar territory.

Athletes of Life understand that to be balanced you must be in good health, that good health requires a relaxed, supple, and open body; that a relaxed, supple, and open body depends on a fluid, evolved, and upbeat emotional life; that a fluid, evolved, and upbeat emotional life depends on a peaceful and calm mind, open to the unexpected. By emptying an over-charged mind, you automatically unblock you emotional stress, so your muscles naturally relax, you liberate you body and put it in a state of well-being.

That is why Athletes of Life fully experience their emotions. They practice this martial art every chance they get. They start by identifying the emotional state they are in, they accept it, even if it goes against their expectations, then they center themselves "here and now" in what they feel. They bounce back dynamically, using the adversity they encounter to attain their objective. To that end, they train assiduously to master their breathing technique, so they can shed passivity that paralyzes their mind and body. This is what is meant by "emotional intelligence" the cornerstone of our program. *Intelligent Emotions Coaching:* to be aware that, when under stress, our ability to interpret a situation becomes dramatically skewed, causing a great deal of inner turmoil and blocking the body energy.

The triad—"head, heart, mind"—constantly interacts to produce the best, most dramatic results. Athletes of Life boost their energy level by making optimal use of the precious tools of mind, emotions and body. They can positively influence a negative state of mind in two ways. They can boost their energy level. Or they can visualize their body being totally relaxed. Both cases involve harnessing emotional energy and its key ingredient: passion.

Passion is the "starter" for any performance. Whether we practice visualization, deep breathing, relaxation, or any other training method or activity, if we lack "visceral" passion, this capacity to "put our "guts" into it," we will get no benefit from the techniques!

Choose "passion," and your dreams will come true! Even your wildest dreams. If there is one thing I learnt as a coach it's that everything is possible! Whatever the field of activity, real champions believe it, breath it and realize it. They are the famous Athletes of Life who, whatever the odds, respond with a big yes: "It is possible!" It is up to you to play the daring card, to be who you are, a human being constantly evolving.

It is up to you to decide!

THE MAIN POINTS OF THIS CHAPTER

I invite you to put into practice, in your everyday life, the action principles that guide the Athlete of Life:

1) Regardless of my activity, I must radiate enthusiasm, access a state of exaltation, in order to excel. As an Athlete of Life, energy flows freely through my body, ready to ignite every gesture, every word and every thought.

2) I know that true leadership is taught by example. Therefore, I must be fired with the determination to use my own emotional energy for passion, not for fear.

3) I manage my emotions harmoniously by constantly practicing this "mental martial art" of the emotions. My task is to convert the heaviness of emotional coagulation into fluid energy that releases my creativity.

4) By respecting my vital needs, I allow emotional energy to flow freely.

5) I take the path of non-resistance: I identify which emotion I feel, then I accept it, even if it goes against my expectations. I then center myself "here and now" in what I feel to bounce back dynamically to attain my objective.

6) My success implies a state of well-being. My balance depends on total vitality, which only exists in a relaxed body, which is in turn the result of an evolved emotional life, requiring a calm mind, open to the unexpected. In fact, when under stress, my interpretation of what happens is dramatically skewed, causing a great deal of internal turmoil and blocking the body energy.

7) Therefore, I can positively influence a negative state of mind by boosting my energy level and/or by visualizing my body being totally relaxed, all being provoked by the emotional energy of passion. By choosing passion, my dreams will come true! "It is possible!", "I am capable of it!", "I deserve it!"

Chapter 7
THE POWER OF THE BODY
The force of vitality

The 15 years I have spent teaching in fitness/wellness around the world have been enriching. I have had the opportunity to meet thousands of men and women of various ages under diverse social and cultural conditions. I gradually managed to introduce a new approach to the body: to treat it as a friend and not wrestle with its imperfections. Harness and cultivate its rich potential instead of undermining it with a multitude of constraints, inflexible obligations or unreasonable controls. What a sublime pleasure it is to embrace every situation and make it an ally! Where there is hardness, resistance, and obstacles, Athletes of Life unhesitatingly choose the power of softness to attain their principal objective: to radiate the well-being that originates in their cells! When they get up in the morning, the first real question they ask themselves is "What can I do today to energize my being? Life is impossible without energy, and for every act I must invest a certain amount of energy."

Athletes of Life are fully aware how important it is to use their energy ecologically. If they are fully conscious when they use their computer, talk on the telephone, or drive their car, they can economize their vital energy by paying attention to their posture and slowing their breathing. Daily mastery of the formula for perfect-health—channel, act, recover—enables them to accomplish much more by cutting down on the number of useless acts that deplete their resources in the long run. They are not overwhelmed by events. They choose to act; not to be acted upon. Present in each moment, they have the exhilarating experience of being guided by their own internal compass. They use everything they find along the way to move easily on their journey and to avoid focusing all their attention on a future destination.

There is a great discovery that all Athletes of Life make: I am a body, and I have ceased to believe that I have a body! This is not just a philosophical reflection; it implies that every cell vibrates with consciousness. I am a vital process: it is up to me to take care of it! No one else can optimize this precious asset. It is entirely my responsibility. To ignore it would be the biggest mistake I could make. To reject the principle would expose me to grave consequences that I would be the first to suffer and, then my professional dreams, as ambitious as they are, would be shattered.

But what is the difference between having a body and being a body? As an athlete, my training was excessive, mechanistic, and performance-oriented. My body and I were engaged in a gargantuan and destructive struggle. I was convinced that I had to conquer my body, but I only succeeded in exhausting it! Then something clicked. There must be another way, I thought. Throughout my teaching career, I explored a wide variety of approaches, including physical education, aerobics, weight training, hip-hop, classical and modern dance, martial arts, different relaxation techniques, and dramatic arts.

An enriching voyage of discovery enabled me to develop, integrate, and perfect an innovative concept combining relaxation, stretching, and attentiveness or concentration: the "Body Mind Stretch." This "energy-building" approach, economizing precious energy, empowers us *to achieve more, by doing fewer needless things.* It is worth repeating: "the energy is wherever I bring my attention to bear."

Athletes of Life's prime objective is to perform every action with a minimum expenditure of energy. Athletes, businesspersons, and artists continually expend an enormous amount of nervous energy. The resulting nervous tension affects their musculature: the body sends the message to tense up. An excessive discharge saturates their body with superfluous nervous energy. When a muscle contracts, the electrical impulse pulsates in the muscle and in the nerves connected to the muscle.

This state of extreme tension leads to digestive, cardiac, and other unbalances. In short, every time a muscle contracts, there is an expenditure of energy. In the absence of healthy management, there will occur an accumulation of muscular contractions that harm organ function. Tense athletes, businesspersons, and artists exhaust themselves day after day because of excessive efforts and rigid mental attitudes, obsessions with "control," masking a state of worry, fear, and doubt.

These people will have big problems: they mistake their current state of disequilibrium for a normal state: the pernicious dependency is triggered, by virtue of the unfortunate tendency to opt for the lifestyle that is familiar to us, thus "normal." Hence the supreme wisdom that attends real change: *to act in a manner unlike our usual manner.* If we are going too fast, we should slow down; if we slouch, we should straighten up; if our shoulders our stiff, we should relax them; if our faces are wrinkled from worry, we should smile; if we are speaking too fast, we should speak more slowly; if we are obsessed about our opinions, we should learn to listen closely to other people; and, above all, if we don't take time to breathe, we should exhale with our whole body!

This is the most important secret available to us at every instant: the power that can be gained by abdominal breathing. Whatever our area of activity, to breathe is to live, to breathe well is to live well! Alas, a thousand times alas, I constantly remark that in sports, business, and the arts—even at the highest levels—the art of living and achieving excellence that excellent breathing represents is the subject of much scorn.

The media are full of articles about stress, pressure, and tension. Yet, officialdom has yet to recognize the virtues of healthy breathing. By and large, breathing isn't taught in the schools. It's a natural bodily function that is sadly neglected by the majority of human beings! However, opting for the complete breath can empower us! And there's no point babbling on and on to stressed-out people about the virtues of deep breathing: in my opinion, it's just theory! It's just not specific enough. We should tell them to EXHALE.

Breathing out is an act of the here and now, in the heat of stress, that lets our organism gradually and spontaneously recover its natural rhythm. Trying to breathe when everything around us is going crazy can only exacerbate, if that were possible, our anxiety. When we breath out consciously, we gradually recover the helm of our existence and slowly establish good inhalation. Sound breathing begins with a deep abdominal exhalation during which we feel our diaphragm contract, expelling stale air from deep inside us. This creates a vacuum which needs to be filled with fresh air through inhalation during which the abdomen rises naturally.

Like a sailboat riding the waves, it descends into the hollow of the wave. This is the exhalation with the navel moving toward the inside of the abdomen; then the sailboat rises on the summit of the wave. This is the inhalation with the navel moving toward the outside of the abdomen. The art of breathing serves as our anchor in every situation. When we master the practice, we can become the master of our existence and of our environment, and never have to struggle under the yoke of circumstances. To breathe fully is to win!

Athletes of Life know the importance of taking care of their energy potential in order to be more effective and not wasting this precious asset. So they are always careful to move economically while contracting a minimum of muscles so that they can become maximally effective. They aim to eliminate the parasitic, superfluous tensions in any given movement. Their breathing is a precious tool. By relaxing their muscles, they automatically relax their organs and soothe their emotions. They are present in the moment, liberated from destructive reflexes that make them react with agitation to events. They practise this martial art of bodily consciousness in every moment.

Like a ballet dancer, a concert pianist, or an Aikido master, Athletes of Life are one with their practise; they become their activity. They are the movement: mind, emotions, and body unite in perfect rhythm, the "present moment." Operating with a minimum of tension in any given movement or action, they excel. They embody "possibility," simply because they have chosen to be. They see possibility in every moment. Athletes of Life perform every activity with the same devotion. They don't subscribe to the harmful dualism according to which activities are considered important or secondary. Nothing is banal. Everything is grist for the mill, empowering them to reach a higher ground. They use everything to construct a more solid, more stimulating edifice of life.

Thanks to their body, Athletes of Life vibrate with an invulnerable enthusiasm. And immeasurable passion comes along with true success! A very well known communications theory underlines the point:
- Only 7% of a message is communicated through words
- 38% is transmitted by what is vibrated through a voice
- 55% is imparted through gestures, looks, and facial expressions
- this means that 93% of a message is purely physiological, a manifestation of the senses, pure sensuality.

Athletes of Life absorb this essential lesson into the deepest part of their being. That is why they dedicate themselves to maintaining the flame of vitality within them, so they can maximize communication with themselves and thus with their environment.

The equilibrium between their mental, emotional, and physical states represents the wellspring of every achievement, of every success, and of every exploit! Only this inner harmony, this sublime synergy ensures the realization of every objective and makes it possible to "go right to the end"; and not just to exist the duration of a competition, season, or spectacular project for some special circumstances before sadly falling into oblivion.

The formula for Athletes of Life is as follows:
• calm mind
• fluid emotion
• supple body

Together they offer exceptional energy potential for performance, for creativity, for joyous spontaneity.

The following recipe does just the opposite:
• troubled mind
• anxious emotional state
• tense body

These emotional states needlessly deplete the store of energy, leading to an increased need for control to reassure ourselves. As a result, the muscles are even more tense and spontaneity, instinctiveness and healthy creativity go out the window.

In this reactive state, muscular injury, physical disease and various kinds of ill being some benign and some grave proliferate, contributing to even greater self-doubt. People so afflicted are even more likely to cling to comments by people around them to justify or reinforce their own value. They're slaves to their daily routine, sliding down the slippery slope of discouragement. Their physiology resonates with the malaise, triggering a dramatic drop in their self confidence; so they have a destructive image of themselves, the image of a loser. The way they enter into relations with other people is marked by desperation and false hope. So, their performances are only a pale reflection of their present state of ill-being.

It's a question of consciousness and choice. Choosing the noblest possibility means having the courage to accept your present state and forging, day by day, a more exhilarating potential for expression. This is the path trod by Athletes of Life. Their cells vibrate with life. It naturally boosts their confidence, permitting them to see a positive and fortunate image of themselves. Their personal relationships are greatly facilitated, since they focus on what they have to give, and not on vain hopes. Thus, as if by magic, their performance level rises, a brilliant reflection of their state of well-being.

With joy and perseverance, you can employ this strategy for success in your daily life! As in art, regular and exalted practice will give your life a little more value, make it a little more effective, and increase your self confidence. The idea is not to wait until you have reached your destination to reap the benefits of success. On the contrary, divide every project into doable tasks that you feel like accomplishing one after the other so that every day you can enjoy the fruit of your labor. Going through each stage with gusto, motivated by a strong desire, you will move step by step along the road to success! You can't fail; the only risk you run is that you may give up too soon, only a few inches from your dream... So, never forget that *only by persevering can you succeed.*

With this mental, emotional, and physical martial art, you can improve your daily performance by enhancing your basic physiological state, thanks to the 7 powers of the Athlete of Life:

- The Power of Confidence
- The Power of Belief
- The Power of Free Will
- The Power of the Present Moment
- The Power of Visualization
- The Power of Emotion
- The Power of the Body.

It's up to you to decide!

THE MAIN POINTS OF THIS CHAPTER

I invite you to put into practice, in your everyday life, the action principles that guide the Athlete of Life:

1) I get to know my body, I gently befriend it. I learn to put into practice the formula for high energy, expressed as:

    channel, act, recover.

2) I relentlessly ask myself the essential question of the Athlete of Life, "what can I do today to energize my being, because without it I lose the power to achieve my goals"…

3) I use my energy economically, enabling me to do less to accomplish much more. My objective is to perform every action with a minimum expenditure of energy. In fact, the harder I try, the more muscular tension I accumulate, which has a negative effect on my organ function. Therefore, I contract a minimum of muscles for a specific action.

4) I have understood the full power of the saying, "to breathe is to live, to breathe well is to live well". The best tool available to me is called EXHALING! Exhaling is an act of the "here and now", in the heat of stress, that lets my organism spontaneously recover its natural rhythm. By relaxing my muscles, I relax my organs and naturally calm my emotions.

5) Every part of my flesh and my cells also vibrate with consciousness. By consciously exhaling I take back control of my life and reestablish good *inspiration*. To breathe fully is to win!

6) To create real change, I act in a manner unlike my usual manner. My body guides me in this learning process. As an Athlete of Life, I perform every activity with the same devotion, liberated from the vicious circle, creator of stress and therefore of failure, consisting of perceiving some activities as important and others as secondary. I follow, step after step, the road to success, by dividing every project into tasks that I approach one after the other with enthusiasm, in order to reap the fruit of my labor at every moment. And I know deep down in my heart that by persevering I can only succeed!

Part Two

OPTIMIZED TRAINING OF THE ATHLETE OF LIFE

W e always come back to one fundamental principle when practicing any sport or art – the quality and quantity of preparation determines the final performance. No athlete, dancer, musician, singer or martial artist can consider being competitive without dedicated training. Each one has understood deep within himself that he must "devote himself" fully without any reservation or cheating above all, and without expecting anything in return…

In fact, just because I have chosen this path does not mean that I will automatically gain victory. In summary, top athletes only spend a very small percentage of their time participating in competitions, sometimes only one to two percent! Therefore, they spend well over ninety percent of their time training. And the same applies to the rehearsals of a musician or a dancer, in relation to the time spent in concert or performing in a show. In all cases we see the same dedication to preparation.

However, what do we observe in our society, whether in the area of work and business, relationships and the family or school and education? We spend almost all our time in "competition"! Only a few inadequate training programs appear here and there to assist us in performance… Romantic relationships and friendships are also weighed down by the burden of excessive competition, the goal being the egotistical satisfaction of gaining something from this exchange, gaining some kind of benefit. Performance has even invaded the intimate sphere of sexuality…

In all areas of life "receiving" prevails and is conveyed by the need to see any exchange as a permanent competition, lacking in interiority: I must be a conqueror to exist in the eyes of others, to maintain my illusion of "controlling" both others and circumstances… And yet, unfortunately, in the areas of sport and artistic activities, the quest for profit at any price has emerged as a corrupting force. The number of competitions, recitals or concerts, has radically increased, opening the door to excesses of all sorts, particularly drug use.

To escape this chaos, the Athlete of Life has decided to consider his life as a gigantic training field, giving him the opportunity to train his own behavior at any time. He has permanently left behind him the social illusion that success will bring him the joy of life essential to every human being. What is in fact the common goal hidden behind these different desires:

- to pass an exam;
- to marry a person you find attractive;
- to set up your own business;
- to go on holiday in the tropics;
- to lose weight, get rid of wrinkles;
- to get an eagerly-awaited pay rise;
- to own a villa in the country;
- to buy a certain make of car;
- to want to win the lottery;
- to clench a big money-making deal;
- to become a millionaire;
- to win this competition...

There is no doubt that behind these types of desire there is an omnipresent, or even obsessive general motivation – "having in order to be successful"!

However, obtaining money, promotion, victory or other devices in no way changes the opinion that I have of myself. The more I obtain, the more I need to obtain to maintain a satisfactory image of myself, an image born of illusion, of course...

This is why the Athlete of Life trains day after day to "be successful" above all as a man or woman. He has understood that his well-being depends above all on his own internal attitude and not everyday circumstances. His personal power comes from this capacity and not from the opinion that others have of him. His work is to paint, at all times, by optimizing his behavior, a fresco of well-being, serenity and pleasure.

His goal is clear: to become the best possible, on a mental, emotional and physical level. Joy is his barometer and it is through feeling joy that he excels in all his activities. If he catches himself not feeling it, he does not lie to himself. Here and now, he reconnects with this beneficial and almost magical state, focusing on his qualities, values, energizing beliefs, respect for his vital needs, his dreams, etc.

His reason for being has become his work, giving and dedication his path. Above all he is guided by his "internal compass", he is a craftsman jeweler of emotional intelligence. Under no circumstances does he try to control his destiny, he knows how to let go and the state of relaxation, calm and serenity becomes his most powerful friend. He has understood that confidence goes hand in hand with the ability to know how to relax. Living in the "here and now" is his credo.

He has learnt to get to know himself, he knows who he is. And it is, almost paradoxically, this state of internal happiness that propels him completely naturally towards a level of high performance. This success that he searched for desperately and frenetically in the past, wasting a huge amount of energy for little benefit, this success now comes to him in abundance, with the greatest detachment… His life has become simple, extremely simple!

Having become genuine and true to himself faced with each choice that he makes, he spontaneously recognizes those who will nurture his vision and those, on the other hand, that have no place in it. Playing has become his place of refuge, playing his life goes hand in hand with sincerity. The Athlete of Life generously nurtures a vision, then decides to put in place a winning strategy to make his hopes reality.

He knows the real reasons that motivate him to pursue this type of goal, he has the capacity to use his talents and all his resources to the full, without forgetting to erase day after day the areas of resistance that try to distance him from his aims. To do this he trains prolifically all the time, day after day, to keep up this work on himself. He continuously builds up a positive image of himself, using his activity, whatever it is, to become a better, free person.

"Those who are courageous, they go headlong.

They search all opportunities of danger. Their life philosophy is not that of insurance companies.

Their life philosophy is that of a mountain climber, a glider, a surfer. And not only in the outside seas they surf; they surf in their innermost seas. And not only on the outside they climb Alps and Himalayas; they seek inner peaks.

But remember one thing – never forget the art of risking, never never. Always remain capable of risking. And wherever you can find an opportunity to risk, never miss it, and you will never be a loser. Risk is the only guarantee for being truly alive."

OSHO

Part Three

ATHLETE OF LIFE:
A PRACTICAL GUIDE

The training takes place in seven phases, each lasting a week. These phases are cumulative; they don't replace one another. So, in the third week, you would practice the exercises from the previous two weeks along with the new ones.

These exercises don't present any particular risk. They can be done by anyone. Nevertheless, the editor and the author decline any responsibility in the event of a physical or health problem.

Week 1

THE POWER OF CONFIDENCE

The force to act

A word from your coach:
Proper breathing builds confidence!

Training: BREATHING

Lying calmly on your back, with your body relaxed and your right hand on your lower abdomen, take the time to feel the natural movement of your breathing, anchored from your center, located 2 inches below the navel.

Exhale deeply, as described below. Your inhalation should begin in your abdomen, proceed to your chest and finish around you shoulders. Then, let the exhalation occur naturally from top to bottom.

Your hand will let you feel the movement of your breathing from your center. Listen to your body, be open, be aware of your inner self, of your bountifulness... complete 3 breathing cycles in a row at least 3 times a day.

Exhalation

Exhalation returns your body to its natural rhythm.

As often as possible during the day, exhale deeply, contracting your diaphragm.

Then, allow a natural inhalation to occur, as indicated above.

Reflection

At the end of the week, set some time aside to reflect.

First, go over the exercise you practiced during the week: reflect on the practical experience that you underwent.

Then draw up a list of SEVEN EXHILERATING THINGS that you have done in your life.

Reminder

As an aid to reflection, you can read the corresponding section in Part One every morning.

Week 2

THE POWER OF BELIEF

The force to believe

A word from your coach:
A supple body means a supple mind.

Training: STRETCHING

Practice the following seven stretching exercises everyday.

Every exercise is done gently, enthusiastically, and with a clear mind, three fundamental qualities that foster suppleness of mind, heart and body!

Do these exercises in a calm pleasant place. Make sure the temperature is suitable for doing this set of energy exercises.

The objective is to center yourself, through your actions, in the present moment. If troubling thoughts arise, simply let them pass without rejecting them. Let go, feeling reassured and confident.

Fill your movements with joy.

Take the time to exhale deeply. Listen to your body. It is your friend and ally. You will progress calmly, your mind, emotions and body will unite in a single expression, here and now.

Hold each position from 20 to 30 seconds. Then let go with a big sigh. Feel the vitality flowing within you.

Exercise 1

Position: standing, knees slightly bent. Fold your hands and gradually stretch your palms up toward the sky. Visualize the space between your vertebrae in order to lighten your spinal disks.

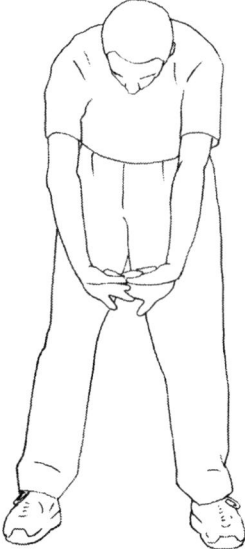

Exercise 2

Position: standing, knees slightly bent. With your hands folded again, slowly and gradually round your back by tilting your pelvis forward, tightening your buttocks, and moving your chin toward your chest. Feel each vertebra move and visualize the space between them.

Exercise 3

a) Position: standing, knees slightly bent. Stretch your right leg forward, slightly bent. With your left hand, hold your right elbow and bring your right arm toward your left shoulder. Stretch.

b) Repeat the exercise on the other side.

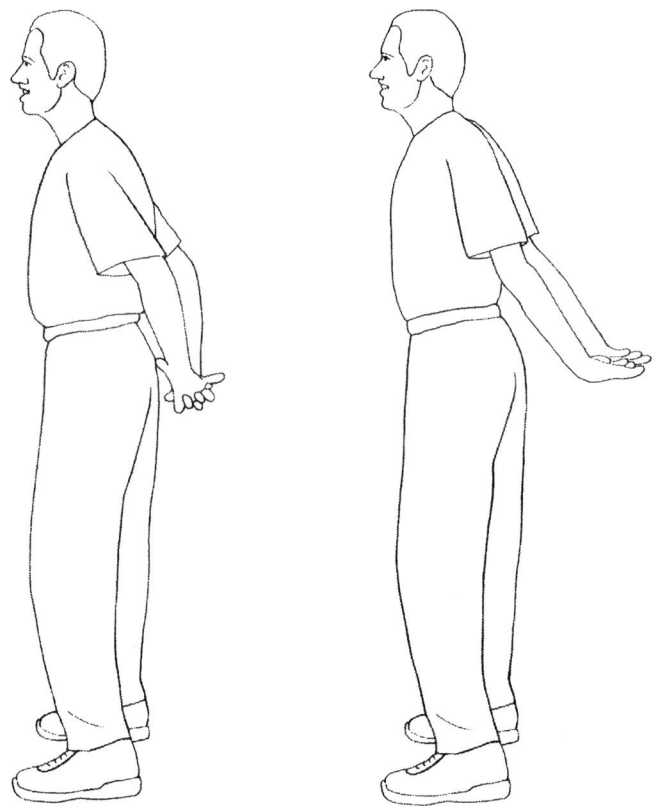

Exercise 4

Position: standing, knees slightly bent, the back straight. Put your arms behind your back, fold your hands, then turn the palms toward the outside. Then if your are comfortable, stretch your arms toward the ground.

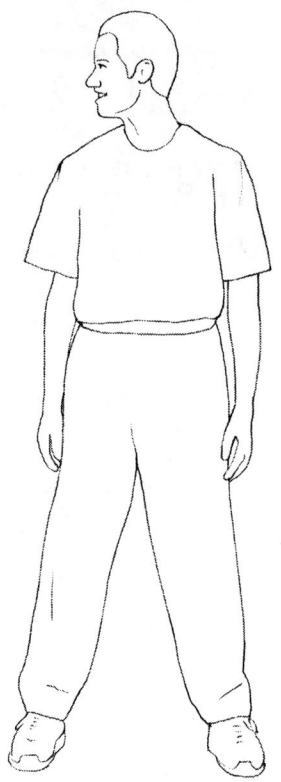 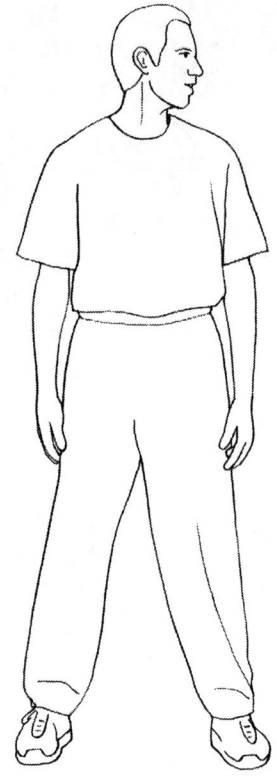

Exercise 5

a) Position: standing, knees slightly bent. Without turning your torso, turn your head slowly to the right.

b) Repeat the exercise on the other side.

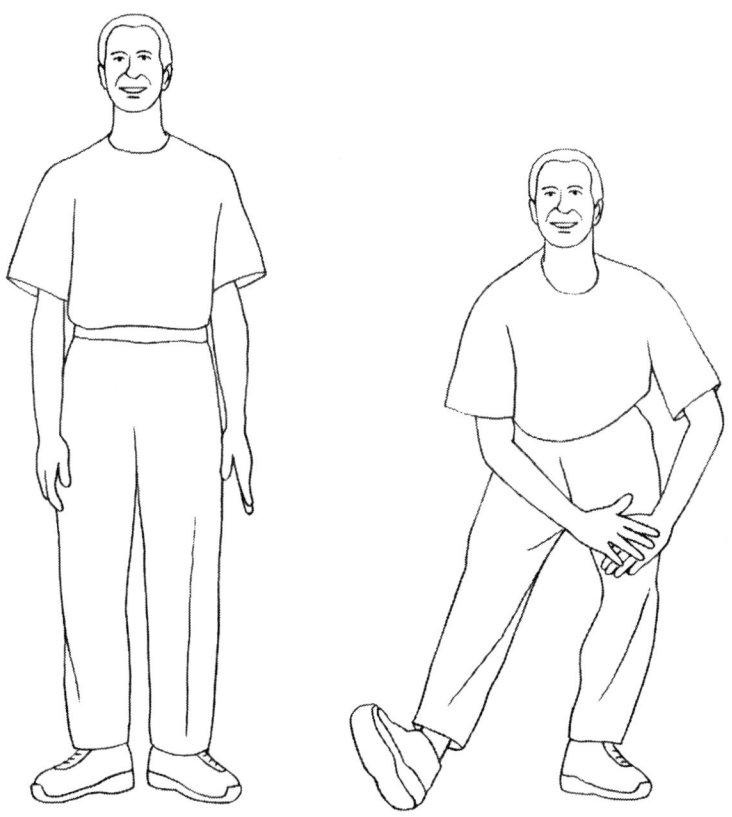

Exercise 6

a) Position: standing, legs together. Turn your feet outside; bend your knees. Slowly stretch your right leg in front of you, lifting your toes up. Put your hands on your left thigh for support, keeping your back straight. Gently return to the starting position.

b) Repeat the exercise on the other side.

Exercise 7

a) Position: standing, legs together. Slowly bend your right knee bringing your right heal toward your buttocks. Keep your feet parallel. Gently return to the starting position.

b) Repeat the exercise on the other side.

Reflection

At the end of the week, set some time aside to reflect.

First, go over the exercises you practiced during the week: reflect on the practical experience that you underwent.

Then draw up a list of SEVEN POSITIVE EVENTS that life has offered you.

Reminder

As an aid to reflection, you can read the corresponding section in Part One every morning.

Week 3

The Power of Free Will

The force to decide

A word from your coach:
Calmness improves your decision making.

Training: RELAXATION

Every day, do a session of relaxation, as follows:

Lie calmly on your back and observe your breathing. Breathe from the abdomen, naturally, like a newborn baby. With each exhalation, think "calming, relaxing," allowing your body to become more and more relaxed. "Let your attention rest on the energy flowing through your body."

Relax your scalp... Relax the muscles of your forehead, the area around your nose, your eyes and your cheeks. Relax your jaw, then your neck. Release your tongue from your pallet. Feel your entire body relax.

Let the weight fall off your shoulders onto the floor. Then relax your arms all the way to your fingertips. Relax your chest. Feel the movement near your sternum. Your rib cage opens and closes like an accordion. Feel your abdomen rise and fall freely, giving a deep massage to your organs.

Relax your hips, the front of your thighs, your knees, the area around your tibias, all the way to your toes. Relax your ankles.

Note the weight of your calves, and the back of your thighs. Completely relax your buttocks, and let your lower back sink pleasantly to the ground.

Surrender your back to the floor like a drop of oil spreading over a sheet of glass. Notice the state of relaxation of your face which is as open as a child's.

Mentally go over every part of your body, appreciating every point of tension relaxing all your muscles. Take the time to enjoy this moment of tranquility, feeling the billions of cells in your body regenerating you. Let yourself go voluptuously into the present moment, here and now.

Then use a specific assertion such as:
"I am getting calmer and calmer every day."
"I am confident."
"I am daring."
Inhale and say: "I am confident."
Exhale: "I see it, I feel it, I believe it."

Let go and feel the energy flowing in your body. Then consciously come back to where you are. Gently move your fingers, and your toes. Slowly stretch your whole body, keeping your eyes closed. Follow your breathing: abdomen-chest-shoulders.

Exhale deeply; swallow your saliva; make grimaces; stretch, and then calmly open your eyes.

Reflection
At the end of the week, set some time aside to reflect.

First, go over the exercises you practiced during the week: reflect on the practical experience that you underwent.

Then draw up a list of SEVEN JUDICIOUS CHOICES that have enriched your life.

Reminder

As an aid to reflection, you can read the corresponding section in Part One every morning.

Week 4

THE POWER
OF THE PRESENT MOMENT

The force of attentiveness

A word from your coach:
To be aware of your body is to live in the now.

Training: QUESTIONS-AFFIRMATIONS

As often as possible ask yourself THESE THREE "Questions-Affirmations":

Question 1: "Am I relaxed?"

Action 1: "Here and now, I relax each of my muscles and free myself of all tension."

Question 2: "Am I exhaling deeply?"

Action 2: "Here and now, I breath out as deeply as possible."

Question 3: "Am I moving gracefully and am I expressing myself confidently?"

Action 3: "Here and now, I am moving gracefully and expressing myself tactfully."

Reflection

At the end of the week, set some time aside to reflect.

First, go over the exercises you practiced during the week: reflect on the practical experience that you underwent.

Then draw up a list of SEVEN EXCITING ELEMENTS IN YOUR LIFE TODAY.

Reminder

As an aid to reflection, you can read the corresponding section in Part One every morning.

Week 5

THE POWER OF VISUALIZATION

The force of images

A word from your coach:
Use your creativity to anticipate precisely.

Training: MENTAL IMPRINTING

Bodily relaxation and positive mental assertions are key factors in this phase.

Perform the same steps as were described in week 3. You have now mastered them and they help you relax quite quickly.

You are going to visualize your dream. You will imagine that your objective has been reached. The aim is to see and feel yourself with a new potential for expression. It is absolutely fundamental "to visualize viscerally" the desired situation.

To see it in all its details with its clear shape, contrasting colors, a lot of light... To hear it, to perceive it, to "taste it," to touch it... To feel it resonate and vibrate throughout your body!

As we have seen, our unconscious makes no distinction between an imagined experience and a real one! That is what gives it its power during this training!

Reflection
At the end of the week, set some time aside to reflect.

First, go over the exercises you practiced during the week: reflect on the practical experience that you underwent.

Then draw up a list of SEVEN "FAR FETCHED PROJECTS" THAT YOU WOULD LIKE TO CARRY OUT.

Reminder

As an aid to reflection, you can read the corresponding section in Part One every morning.

Week 6

THE POWER OF EMOTION

The force of enthusiasm

A word from your coach:
Pleasure produces performance!

Training: ANCHORING-VERTICALITY

You are now going to develop your ability to anchor your body, thus improving your awareness.

Keep your spinal column vertical. Your chin is slightly in, your neck straight, your shoulders relaxed, and your feet rooted in the ground.

Throughout the day, note the quality of your verticality.

Reflection

At the end of the week, set some time aside to reflect.

First, go over the exercises you practiced during the week: reflect on the practical experience that you underwent.

Then draw up a list of SEVEN EVENTS, MEETINGS OR MOMENTS DURING WHICH YOU FELT AN EMOTIONAL "EXPANSION" OF ENTHOUSIASM.

Reminder

As an aid to reflection, you can read the corresponding section in Part One every morning.

Week 7

THE POWER OF THE BODY

The force of vitality

A word from your coach:
You "are" the rhythm!

Training: PYRAMID WALK

As often as possible, go for a walk and adjust your breathing to the rhythm of your steps. Do so, gently and progressively to improve your cardiovascular capacities. Exhale for three steps, inhale for 3 steps, then for 4 steps, 5 steps, 6 steps, then based on your training and the length of the walk, you may manage 8, even 12 steps. Then start decreasing the number of steps per breath until you reach 3.

If you have not yet reached your destination, maintain a 3/3 rhythm, or 4/4 if it suits you better.

On another walk, you'll perform the exercise for the odd numbers only (For example, 3, 5, 7, 9, 7, 5, 3).

Take advantage of the occasion to enjoy your training!

Reflection
At the end of the week, set some time aside to reflect.

First, go over the exercises you practiced during the week: reflect on the practical experience that you underwent.

Then draw up a list of SEVEN POSITIVE MESSAGES THAT YOUR BODY GIVES YOU.

Reminder

As an aid to reflection, you can read the corresponding section in Part One every morning.

ACKNOWLEDGEMENTS

*To all the people, the world over, who have had confidence
in me and have believed in my work, whether through
my books or our Intemo® training and coaching programs.
Thank you for being the embodiment of the Athlete of Life,
throughout your everyday life!*

Thank you also to:

all the team at Éditions Un monde différent,

Marc Maillard, Vincent Buffet,

Thierry Barnerat,

Tonino Vaccaro and the Fade-In Studio,

Sonja K.,

René Camenzind and Jean-Jacques Crettaz,

Mike and Cathy Horn,

My family,

Little Thérèse.

THIERRY SCHNEIDER

Thierry Schneider has written several successful books including *Vivre grand* (*Living Big*), *Cœur à cœur* (*Heart to Heart*), *Joy, tout est possible!* (*Joy, everything is possible*) and *Mon corps, rebelle ou ami?* (*My body, friend or enemy?*) on his path to the Athlete of Life. A path that he invites you to follow with this work, a summary of this whole approach and a real "guide" intended for anyone who has decided to "make a go of it".

Thierry Schneider is the European leader in coaching and mental preparation, himself a true "Athlete of Life". He coaches, on an international level, businesspeople, top athletes, trainers and artists, helping them obtain their level of excellence.

Since 1997 he has been able to develop his method due to the vision and experience of a former adult education and training manager Marc Maillard, now a consultant and professional coach, with whom he formed a partnership to create Intemo®.

Intelligent Emotions™

The *Natural creative process*, devised by Thierry Schneider and distributed exclusively by *Intemo*®, gives you the means to achieve your most ambitious goals and become an "Athlete of Life"!

It is comprised of individual coaching, in-house training, team coaching and public courses. Furthermore, every year, a passionate group of people train with us, to obtain our license, either to benefit their business and/or to become partners and teach our method.

Why wait to put into action the projects you feel strongly about?

Contact us!

E-mail: intemo@intemo.ch

Web site: www.intemo.ch

Sign up to receive Thierry's message free of charge every month: "Athlete of Life"!